# Allied Attack Boats

A Study of the Storm
and Assault Boats
Used in River Crossings
in Europe During
World War II

TRAVELOGUE 219

John Sliz

Copyright © 2013 Travelogue 219
All rights reserved. No part of this book may be reproduced, stored in a retrieval system, or transmitted in any form without the written permission of the publisher.

ENG-2 Allied Attack Boats: A Study of Storm and Assault Boats Used in River Crossing in Europe in World War II, January 2013
Published by: Travelogue 219
        Toronto, Canada
ISBN 978-0-9877404-9-6

Unless otherwise noted, all charts and drawings by John Sliz

Front cover main photo taken by author. Other photos are credited elsewhere in this book.

**Thank you** to Philip Reinders,, Bill McVean, Ken Holmes, and Laura Sliz.

It is my best intention to honour the men of the engineers of all countries by accurately recording their accomplishments. If you think that I have misquoted anyone, gotten anything wrong or have more information please let me know via my website.

www.stormboatkings.ca

A note on spelling: in most cases I went with British Standard and left all quotes exactly as they were recorded to reflect the nationality of the speaker.

# Contents

Glossary .................................................................... iv
The Reason For This Book ................................................. 1
The Need For Army Boats .................................................. 3
U.S. Small Boats ........................................................... 5
Assault Boats .............................................................. 7
Storm Boats ............................................................... 21
Pneumatic Floats .......................................................... 25
British And Commonwealth ................................................ 27
British Assault Boats ..................................................... 29
Storm Boat Mark I ........................................................ 34
Motors ..................................................................... 41
Johnson Sea-Horse POLR-15 .............................................. 43
Motor, Outboard, 50 H.P Model 8008 ..................................... 45
Seagull Engine Mark III ................................................... 50
Conclusion ................................................................. 54
End Notes ................................................................. 56
References ................................................................. 57
About The Author .......................................................... 58

# Glossary

| | |
|---|---|
| B.H.P. | British Horse Power |
| | |
| C.E. | Chief Engineer. |
| Class 9 | A designation for a bridge that can take loads up to and including 9 tons (ie. most medium trucks and cars) |
| CO | Commanding officer |
| Coy | Company |
| CRE | Commander Royal Engineers |
| Cwt | Hundredweight |
| | |
| Div | Division |
| DUKW | An amphibious truck |
| | |
| E.B.E. | Experimental Bridging Establishment |
| | |
| F.B.E. | Folding Boat Equipment mostly used for bridging, but was able to transport infantry |
| Fd Pk | Field Park |
| | |
| GHQ | General Headquarters |
| GSO | General Staff Officer |
| | |
| H-hour | Time of attack |
| Hp | Horse Power |
| HQ | Headquarters |
| Hrs | Hours |
| | |
| Lt | Lieutenant |
| | |
| M.E.X.E. | Military Engineering Experimental Establishment |
| m.p.h. | Miles per hour |
| | |
| RAF | Royal Air Force |
| R.C.E. | Royal Canadian Engineers |
| Recce | Reconnaissance |
| RE/R.E. | Royal Engineers |
| | |
| Sapper | The equivalent to a Private in the Engineer Corps |
| SORE | Staff Officer Royal Engineers |
| Strumboot | German Storm boat |
| | |
| USAAF | United States Army Air Force |

# The Reason for This Book

Almost ten years ago, I started my research on the efforts of the 23rd Field Company, Royal Canadian Engineers during Operation Berlin and almost immediately I ran into a problem. There was very little information on the Storm boats that they used to get the British 1st Airborne Division across the Rhine River.

I eventually found the information in the National Archives and Library (Canada), but not before I ran into a lot of confusion online and in books. Unfortunately, there were enough people that swore that Assault boats were Storm boats and vise versa. This put doubt in the true facts when they were presented. To set the record straight I searched in the Canadian archives for all of the boats used by the Royal Canadian Engineers* and wrote `Engineer Assault Boats In Canadian Service'. It was published in 2006 by Service Publications and I thought that was the end of the confusion.

Lately, I have noticed online and in a few high profile publications that there has been a lot of misinformation over American made Assault Boats and Storm Boats, maybe for good reason.

* they used the same water crossing equipment as the Royal Engineers.

There doesn't seem to be anything out there that illustrates what is what. At least until now.

In the following pages, I will illustrate the differences in the types of boats used by the American army and the British and Commonwealth armies in Europe during World War II. I have expanded on what I previously wrote about in `Engineer Assault Boats in Canadian Service' and added more drawings and charts.

The drawings alone will clearly show the differences between all of the equipment used. I have also shown the differences in the distribution and supply of the boats in the field.

Beside Assault Boats and Storm Boats, two other boats must be mentioned. I included the American Pneumatic Float, even though it wasn't meant for direct assault. It was designed for transporting troops in follow up waves and for bridging. The British equivalent—sort of—was the Folding Boat Equipment (F.B.E.), which was designed for bridging, but could be used for ferrying troops. I didn't include the F.B.E. because—as far as I know— it was never used in an assault and I had previously covered the boat in `Engineer Assault Boats In Canadian Service'. Likewise, Reconnaissance boats and pontoons of both countries were not suitable for assault and therefore not within the scope of this book.

The boats covered in this book are:

## American:
Assault Boat M1
Assault Boat M2
Storm Boat
Pneumatic Float

## British And Commonwealth:
Assault Boat Mark I
Assault Boat Mark II
Assault Boat Mark III
Storm Boat Mark I

# The Need For Army Boats

*"The crossing of a water obstacle in the face of opposition is a specialized form of attack involving the closest co-operation between all arms."* from Military Training Pamphlet No. 23 Part VIII. 1942.

Any advancing army can't expect to capture all of the bridges on the route to their objective and this was especially true against an enemy like Germany, who very meticulously destroyed the majority of the bridges during their retreats. To ensure that the advance continued, the infantry had to get across a river to secure a large enough bridgehead for the engineers to construct a bridge that allowed the heavy weapons to cross.

This concept was not new to the armies of the world, but the concept of using powered boats for rapid crossings was. Besides the advantage of speed, outboard motors were also used in rivers where it was thought that the current was too strong for paddled boats. This point was driven home when German engineers demonstrated their efficiency of their river crossing technique, and in particular the use of Strumboot 39 (or Blitzboot), to get infantry across the Rhine River at Colmar in 1940. The French defenders were fooled by the speed of the attacking boats.

Impressed by the use of the speed boats, Lieutenant-Colonel Paul W. Thomspon of the U.S. Army wrote the following quote and it sums up what the Corps of Engineers knew about the German Strumboot at the time: *"The boat apparently is made of light-weight metal (possibly of plywood) and is powered by an outboard motor which appears to have four cylinders and which probably develops upwards of 40 hp. The motor with its long propeller shaft serves also as a rudder for steering the boat. An idea as to the weight of the equipage is gained from a sketch (not reproduced here) which shows six men carrying the boat while four men carry the motor. The capacity of the storm boat appears to be eight men with personal equipment, and the crew. The crew consists of a single Engineer soldier. The storm boat is one of the very items of German Engineer equipment which had not been observed in use prior to the war. It is likely that it was developed especially for the crossing of the Rhine."* [1]

Inspired by the German use of speed boats, both the United States and Britain developed their own version of the storm boat, with the Americans going for top speed while the British preferred a heavier payload. Until then both groups had relied on their own versions of assault boat, and their mark I designs were similar in size and appearance. The main difference was that the British version was collapsible while the American version was solid. It was when the second and third marks came along that the designs really differed.

The Assault Boats were the armies' main boat and each division and/or corps carried a small amount of them that the engineers could have at their disposal. Storm boats were held at the Army level and required special training to operate them.

Above: An U.S. Assault Boat M1 with an outboard motor during the building of a bridge. The M1 handled a motor better than the M2 version. From a Signal Corps' Postcard.
(author's collection)

# U.S. Small Boats

In the fall of 1940 a number of committees were assigned to study river crossing tactics at a research course and expressed considerable dissatisfaction with the equipage available and urged that much could be learned from German practices. The following was stated in one of the committees' reports: *"The few seconds—or even minutes—of additional secrecy after the first wave leaves our shore is of relatively small value...In any case, the first burst of fire, when the enemy first discovers one of our boats, gives away the show; if by the use of fast motor boats we can be down his throat within seconds after he discovers us, we are better off than if we have to paddle laboriously to the shore in the face of fire."* [2]

Besides their recommendation for Storm boats, they also mentioned rubber boats. They had seen pictures of German troops using pneumatic floats as assault boats and ferries as early as 1933. What they thought of them at the time wasn't much, but as tests confirmed their value opinions changed. One advantage they started to see was that the rubber boats were easier to transport.

In 1941, Lieutenant-Colonel Lumsford G. Oliver, Chief Engineer of I Armoured Corps, wrote, *"I have always thought of our assault boats as being superior to the rubber boats, but have changed my mind...thinking the use of the large rubber boats."* [3]

In 1940, the United States Army in World War II grouped their small boats into two classes: paddle boats and powerboats, even though outboard motors were attached to paddle boats with various results. The Assault Boat M1 was the Army's main boat at the time and it fit into both categories.

Army tactics at the time dictated, if paddleboats were used for the initial assault, the assault was usually made during darkness to gain surprise and to prevent, to quote a report, *"...the boats being mowed down like sitting ducks."* [4]

At the start of the war, only the Assault Boat Mark I was being produced and in 1940, only one out of a total of four potential suppliers was awarded a contract over $100,000 to produce the boats for the army.[5] By the end of the year all of the 2,456 Assault boats required by the army had been delivered. The number grew to 3,446 the following year. Production then shifted the next year to: *Assault, M2, without paddles or canvas bag* and the figures grew to 14,680 boats being made. This number was 2,761 boats above the requirement.

Deliveries of the *Assault, M2, without paddles or canvas bag* in 1943 amounted to 19,899, which was 174 boats above the requirement. Only 377 boats were needed in 1944 and this order was easily filled. Of the 15,462 boats required in the last year of the war only 2,657 were delivered.

The figures for Storm boats or *Storm, plywood*, as it is listed, start in 1942 as 1,131, 359 boats below the 1490 required. By December 1943 the figure amounted to 1,407 boats, which was 15 boats over the requirement. There were no deliveries in 1944 and 2,502 boats were delivered in 1945, well below the 5,782 required. According to the Corps' history, the supply of boats was satisfactory; it was a lack of engines to supply them that was the problem.

## Production By Year

| Year | A.B. M1 | A.B. M2 | Storm Boat | Pneumatic 10 man |
|---|---|---|---|---|
| 1940 | 2,456 | 0 | 0 | 0 |
| 1941 | 3,446 | 0 | 0 | 0 |
| 1942 | 0 | 14,680 | 1,131 | 0 |
| 1943 | 0 | 19,899 | 1,407 | 820 |
| 1944 | 0 | 377 | 0 | 1,238 |
| 1945 | 0 | 2,657 | 2,502 | 3,710 |
| Total | 5902 | 37,613 | 5,040 | 5,768 |

Note: all figures are from: *United States Army In World War II The Technical Services. The Corps of Engineers: Troops And Equipment* by Blanche D. Coll, Jean E. Keith and Herbert H. Rosenthal. Office of the Chief of Military History. Department of the Army. Washington, D.C. 1958

At the end of the war, their main paddle boat was the Assault boat M2 and their powerboat was the Storm boat. Both boats were still in use during the Korean Conflict and it wasn't until 1955 that there were plans to replace the Assault Boat M2 with the fiberglass T3 Assault Boat that could handle motors a lot better than the Assault Boat M2. The production cost of each boat in September 1954 was $249.18 for the Assault Boat M2 and $415.97 for the Storm Boat.[6]

# Assault Boats

Assault Boat M1:

The Assault Boat M1 was, to quote a training publication from the Infantry School, *"...of the flat bottom skiff type."* [6] It was 13'-4" long, 5 feet in beam, and weighed 200 pounds. The skin was made of fir plywood ½ inch thick; the ribs, gunwales, skids, and slot flooring were oak. The publication also stated that, *"Seven ordinary canoe paddles are provided for propelling the boat when fully loaded. Two men can paddle it when empty. It is provided with a carrying rail to assist the men in carrying it. Ordinarily, a crew of two engineers will be provided with each boat, one paddling in the stern in order to steer the boat, and the other in the bow as stroke. These two engineers and five of the infantry passengers paddle when the boat is fully loaded; the two engineers can return the empty boat from its first trip for another load. With the men fully equipped, the assault boat will safely carry any one of the loads indicated in Table II. (see page 14) The capacity loads listed are exclusive of two engineers who assist in paddling the boat and who remain with the boat to take it back across the stream for additional loads."* [7]

According to the Engineer Soldier's Handbook, the boat could be easily carried by four men who utilized the hand grips on the gunwales: *"Care must be taken not to drag the bottom on the ground, or bump the boat against stumps and trees."* [8]

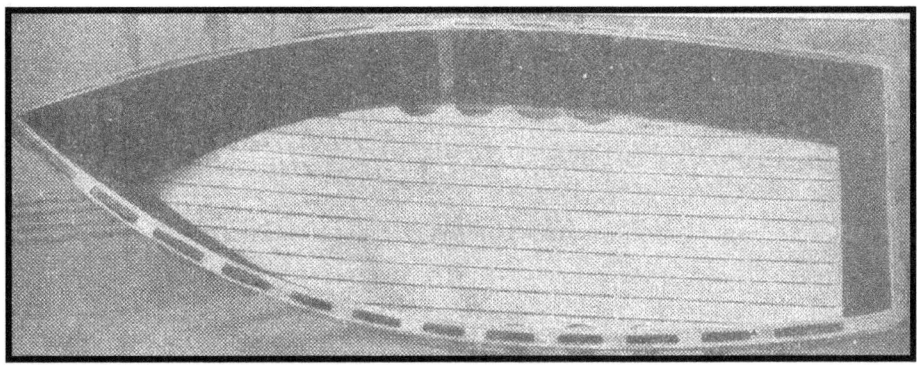

Above left: Top view of an Assault Boat M1.
(from FM 21-105 Engineer Soldier's Handbook, U.S. Army 2 June 1943)

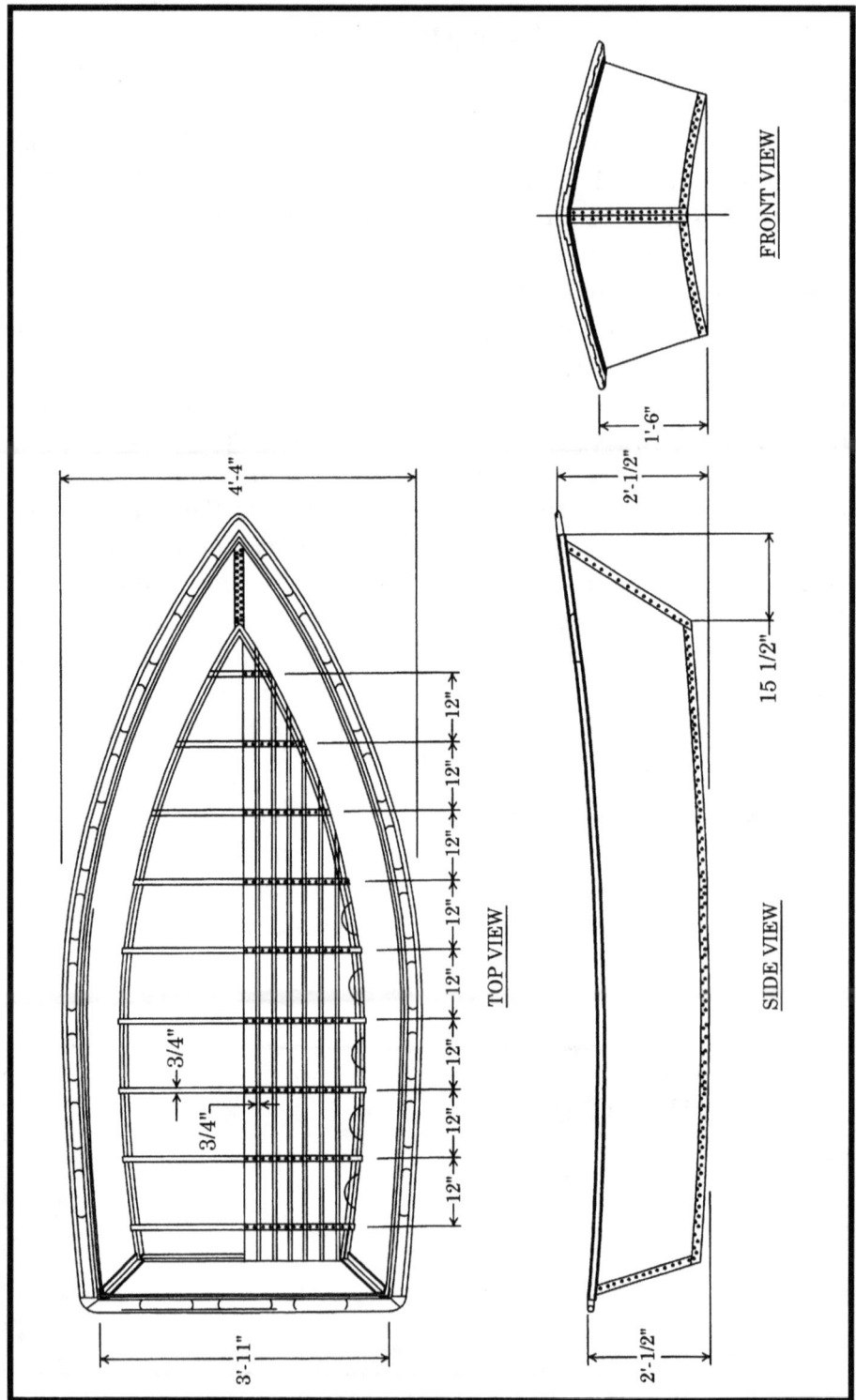

**U.S. Assault Boat M1**

A training article, *'Engineers in a River Crossing'*, lists the standard practice in moving from the forward assembly area to the river as:

1) *Passengers and crew assigned to a boat should carry the boat in a continuous forward movement by the most direct route (previously reconnoitered) from the forward assembly area at the water.*

2) *All boats of the initial wave should arrive at the river bank at the same time (H hour).*

3) *Every precaution should be taken to prevent noise; the boat should not be allowed to strike its sides or bottom while in transit to the water; paddles should be carried by hand.*

4) *Upon arrival at the river bank and before being loaded, the boat should be carried, bow first, into the water.*

5) *Individual boats should be kept well separated along the front of the crossing unit. No attempt is made to maintain any specific formation or line while in the water. Care should be taken to avoid hitting the sides of the boat with paddles and to avoid splashing. Any passengers not paddling should crouch low in the boat and not shift positions during the crossing. There should be no firing from the boat. Upon arrival at the far bank, passengers lay their paddles in the boat, disembark, unload any extra equipment and ammunition expeditiously, and continue their missions. The engineer crew then paddles the boat back for the next load.*[9]

The time required for paddling the Assault Boat M1 across a river of moderate current was about one minute for a width of 100 yards and about three and one-half minutes for 300 yards. The time required to return the assault boat to the near bank, load, and recross to the far shore depended upon the amount of confusion in unloading at the far bank when the first wave

Next page: an Associated Press photo that was published in newspapers in the USA on September 4th 1942 with the caption: *'Rangers In Training-A rugged type of combat soldier is being developed at a Pacific Northwest Army camp– Combat Engineer– is shown here in a stream-crossing exhibition that is part of their regular training.'* (author's collection)

landed the dispersion of the boats upon their return to the near bank, and the time required to load the second wave. It usually amounted to several times the actual paddling time.

The drift in a current of one mile per hour on a boat being paddled at right angles to the current of the river, which was one hundred yards pushed the boat thirty-five yards downstream of where they originally set off from. This did not affect the time it took to cross the river. However it did take longer to cross if the boat was paddled at an angle of forty-five degrees to the current. Whether to allow the drift to save time or to reduce the drift to increase the time it took to cross the river, was the decision of the tactical commander.

## Types of Engineer Units And Equipment Which May Be Available To An Infantry Division For A River Crossing

| Unit | Equipment | Quantity of equipment per unit |
|---|---|---|
| Combat battalion (triangular infantry division) | Assault boats. | 10 |
| Combat battalion (two in each corps) | Assault boats<br>Footbridge equipage | 30<br>1 unit (432 feet) |
| Light Pontoon Company (several in army or GHQ reserve) | Assault boats<br>Footbridge equipage<br>Light pontoon equipage | 80<br>3 units (1296 feet)<br>36 light pontoon boats and equipment |
| Heavy Pontoon Battalion (in GHQ reserve) | Heavy pontoon equipage | 48 heavy pontoon boats and equipment |

## Distribution

All ten of the boats were nested together and were carried in one 1 ½ ton truck. This constituted the only river crossing equipment in the engineer battalion (18 officers and 616 enlisted men in 1942) and hence, the infantry division. For a river crossing it was usually necessary to reinforce the engineer battalion with engineers from higher echelons.

In each army corps there were two combat regiments, which were motorized. Each regiment consisted of 39 officers and 1228 enlisted men divided into a regimental headquarters, a headquarters and service company and two battalions of engineers. Seven 1 ½ ton trucks were required to move the regiment's compliment of 30 assault boats and footbridge. These engineers were trained in ferrying and in the construction of both foot and pontoon bridges.

The light pontoon company consisted of 6 officers and 215 enlisted men and was organically an army or GHQ reserve unit, assigned to a Corps or division. The structure was a headquarters and three bridge platoons. In the headquarters platoon was a headquarters section and service section, an assault boat section of eight 1 ½ ton trucks carrying 10 boats each and a footbridge section of eight 1 ½ ton trucks. Each bridge platoon transported one unit of light pontoon bridge equipment on 6 4-ton 4x4 semi-trailer trucks, four 4-ton 6x6 trucks and four 2-wheel trailers.

The heavy pontoon battalion of 12 officers and 462 enlisted men is organically a GHQ reserve unit. Divided into a battalion headquarters, a headquarters and service company and two heavy pontoon bridge companies of two platoons each. Each of the four bridge platoons transported materiel for the construction of one unit of heavy pontoon bridge on 16 semi-trailer, 4 ton, 4x4 trucks. Activities of the battalion were usually confined to the transportation of its equipment and the maintenance of bridges in use.[10]

## Assault Boat Mark I

| Number of Men | Equipment | Ammunition |
|---|---|---|
| 9 | Rifles and individual equipment | 136 rounds per rifleman<br>320 rounds per automatic rifle |
| 8 | 1 light machine gun | 20 boxes of ammunition (5000 rounds) |
| 8 | 1 heavy machine gun | 13 boxes of ammunition (3250 rounds) |
| 7 | 1 81mm mortar | 50 rounds of ammunition |
| 7 | 1 60mm mortar | 150 rounds of ammunition |
| 7 | Equipment of the communication section (forward echelon of a battalion headquarters) | |

## Assault Boat Mark II

| Number of Men | Equipment | Ammunition |
|---|---|---|
| 12 | Rifles and individual equipment | 136 rounds per rifleman<br>320 rounds per automatic rifle |
| 10 | 2 light machine guns | 20 boxes of ammunition (5000 rounds) |
| 7 | 1 heavy machine gun .30 caliber | 13 boxes of ammunition |
| 7 | 1 heavy machine gun .50 caliber | 13 boxes of ammunition |
| 7 | 1 81mm mortar | 50 rounds of ammunition |
| 10 | 2 60mm mortar | 72 rounds of ammunition |
| 8 | Infantry communication platoon wire section with complete equipment. | |

Above: a museum display of an Assault Boat Mark II. (Philip Reinders)

Assault Boat M2:

By 1943, the M1 had been superseded by the M2 and this version was 13'-4" long, 5'-9" wide with a depth of 2'-1". It weighed 410 pounds, displaced 5300 pounds with a freeboard of 4" and 4000 pounds with a freeboard of 8". The sides were 7/16" mahogany plywood, the bottom was 3/8" fir plywood and the transom was 3/4" fir plywood. The corner edges of the bottom sides, and ends of the boat were bound with brass angle-strips, which were fastened to the boat with screws and rivets. The inside of the bottom was covered with a flooring of oak slats attached to the frames. The strip skids, fixed to the bottom for protection during loading and transport, were made of oak. The boats were painted olive drab.[11]

A three-man crew was needed to operate the Assault Boat M2. One man steered at the stern and two paddled on each side, approximately at midpoint.

The Assault boat M2 fit into the paddle boat class and did not perform well when a motor was attached.

Ten to twelve combat-equipped soldiers were required to carry the boat, special weapons, equipment and ammo. The boat was carried inverted until a point 100 to 200 yards from the water and was then turned over and carried upright to the water's edge and launched.

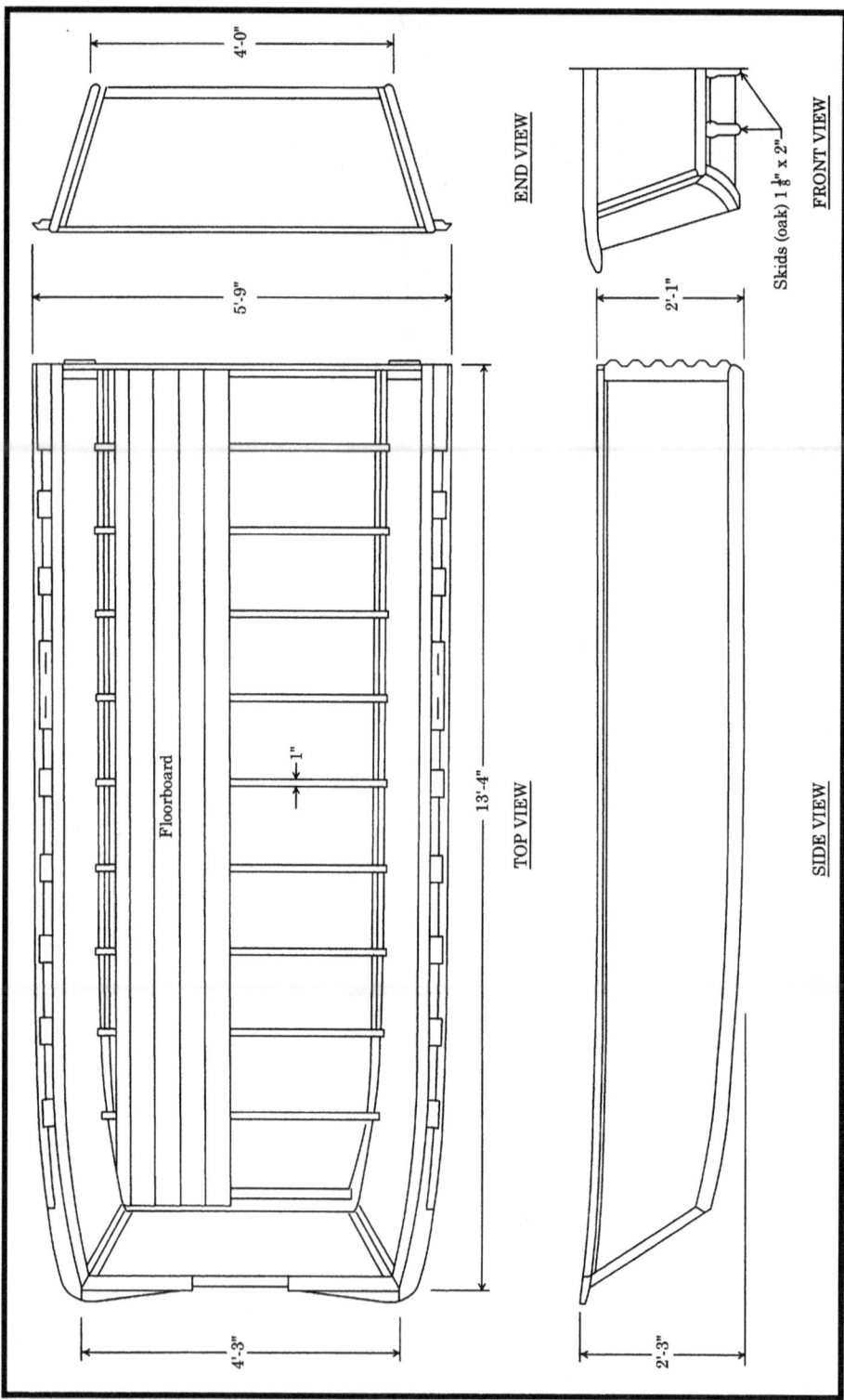

Above: The Assault Boat M2. Redrawn by author from a training manual.

Above: A view of a display of an Assault Boat Mark II in a museum in Luxembourg. Taken by the author. The numbers read:
        7E    ASSAULT BOAT    B-48
           WT. 424  PKG 3/42
               CU.FT.163.1
             DIM. 161X70X32

Above: The Assault Boat Mark II showing a three man engineer team with a twelve man infantry squad.
(from FM 21-105 Engineer Soldier's Handbook, U.S. Army 2 June 1943)

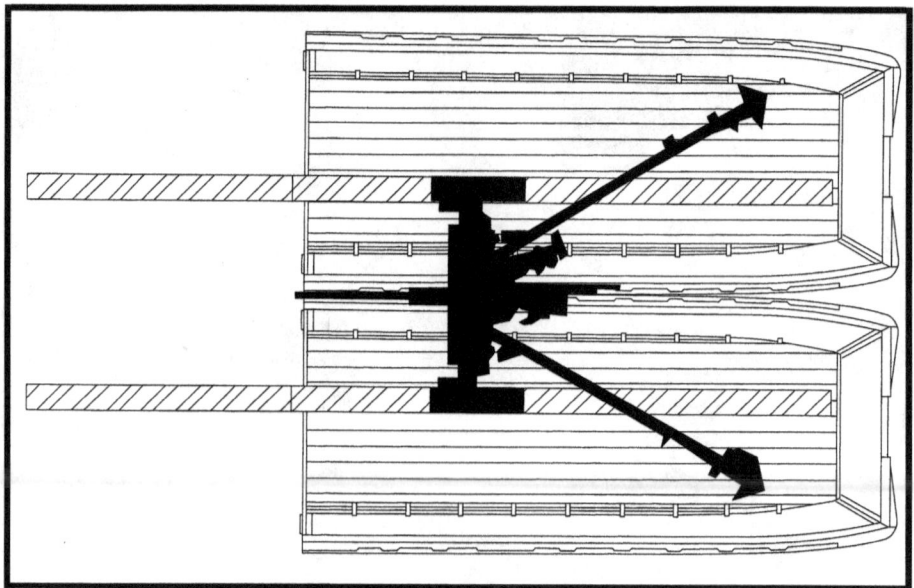

Above: a top view drawing of a 37mm anti-tank gun loaded onto two Assault Boat M2 with ramps still in the loading position. The three engineers and five gun crewmen would paddle on either side of the gun, four per side.

Unlike the British made Assault boat, a single Assault boat was not capable of ferrying an antitank gun as the weapon was too heavy and bulky. However, if two boats were lashed together they were capable of carrying a 37mm anti-tank gun with its five man crew, plus 3 man engineer crew and at least 100 rounds of ammo. The gun sat in the middle while four men on each side paddled. This is not to be confused with the Double Assault Boat.

Double Assault Boat

The sterns of two boats were attached with vertical pins through hinge leafs located on each side of the stern to form a pontoon for bridging. It also was used as a troop carrier known as the Double Assault Boat. A motor was attached to the bow of one boat and that became the stern of the two boat configuration. Unlike the single boat, which was unstable with a motor, this configuration performed well, especially during the Rhine crossing.

This boat could carry twenty-two men. In rough water it was recommended that it carry only fifteen men with a crew of three. [12]

Allied Attack Boats

## Assault Boat Data

| Description | Assault Boat M1 | Assault Boat M2 | Assault Boat M3 (tentative) |
|---|---|---|---|
| **Single boat:** | | | |
| Over-all length | 13'-4" | 13'-4" | 18'-3" |
| Maximum width | 5'-1/2" | 5'-9" | 5'-8" |
| Depth | 1'-8" | 2'-1" | 2'-7" |
| Bow | Pointed | Slightly tapered | Round |
| Stern | Square, sloping | Square | Round |
| Bottom | Flat | Flat | Flat |
| Weight | 200 lb. | 440 lb. | 285 lb. |
| Displacement | 3,200 lb. (6" freeboard) | 4,500 lb. (6" freeboard) | 4,100 lb. (6" freeboard) |
| Paddles | 7 | 9 | 9 |
| **2 boat pontoon:** | | | |
| Over-all length | | 26'-8" | |
| Maximum width | | 5'-9" | |
| Weight | | 880 lb. | |
| Paddles | | 18 | |
| **Capacity:** | | | |
| **Single boat:** | | | |
|   Crew | 2 | 3 | 3 |
|   Passengers | 9 | 12 | 12 |
| **2 boat pontoon** | | | |
|   Crew | | 3 | |
|   Passengers | | 22 [1] | |
| **Maximum safe stream velocity:** [2] | | | |
| **Single boat:** | | | |
|   Trained men | 2 1/2 | 1 1/2 to 2 mph [3] | 3 1/2 to 4 mph |
|   Untrained men | Dangerous in any current | Dangerous in any current | 3 mph |
| **2 boat pontoon:** | | | |
|   Trained men: | | | |
|     With 18 paddles | | 5 mph | |
|     With outboard motor | | 6 1/2 mph [4] | |
|   Untrained men | | Dangerous in any current | |

1 Handles best with 18 me, including crew.
2 Safety factor of about 1/2 mph.
3 3 1/2 mph if total of 12 men.
4 With 220-pound load (1 operator and 50 pounds of fuel) maximum speed is 15.4 mph.

Above: a comparative chart of all the versions of the Assault Boat. Note that the M3 was never in service.

Left: attaching a Double Assault Boat M2 or an Assault Boat Pontoon as it is known when used for bridging. For troops it could be paddled or a 22 hp motor could be attached to either end. (ST 5-260-1B)

Left: a Assault Boat M2 carrying a 7-man 81mm mortar squad complete a 3-man engineer crew, mortar and 50 rounds of ammunition.

Below: a Double Assault Boat with 25hp mortar probably taken post-war.

Bottom: a Storm Boat with twin Johnson 25hp, which was its engine of choice after the war.

## U.S. Storm Boats

The U.S. Storm Boat was a rugged assault raft designed to transport troops assigned to the mission of securing the first objectives in a deliberate river-crossing operation. The boat's main advantage over the other boats was in crossing wide rivers (over 500') or where speed was more important than security.

It was an extremely rugged boat built of high-strength plywood, with internal bracing consisting of a keel and a series of frames extending from the keel to the sides in herring bone fashion. It had a tapered bow and a blunt stern. Additional strength was obtained by a double bottom that was divided into a number of watertight compartments. It was also reinforced by a series of scuffing strips. It was 16'-9" long, 6'-6" at its widest point and had a depth of 1'-10". Without a motor the boat weighed 440 pounds and had a max. safe loading of 1,860 pounds.[13]

The flat bottom boat fit into the powerboat class and was built for speed. Its large (for the time period) 50 horsepower Evinrude motor with special bracket could propel seven men and a crew of two quickly across any

Above: two Assault Boats are in the foreground with Storm Boats behind them in the Minnitonka Boat works. Inset: a Storm boat being carried by the men who built it.

river and beach at full speed. The boat could carry 1500 pounds with very little reduction in speed. [14]

The boat accelerated rapidly and all passengers had to crouch, kneel or lie in the boat and grip the gunwale securely as it started. The normal speed of the Storm Boat with passengers and crew was 20 to 23 miles per hour.

Four boats were nested together and transported on a *2 1/2 ton, utility, pole-type trailer.* The motors were carried in the truck.

With an engineer leading the way, eight men were usually assigned to carry the Storm Boat with motor attached. The motor could also be attached at the water's edge.

The water had to be at least three feet deep at the point of embarkation. The two engineer crew members held the boat steady as the men loaded. The occupants laid on the floor on both sides of the boat facing the bow, taking care to stay clear of the area immediately in front of the motor. The bowman was positioned in

| \multicolumn{3}{c}{Storm Boat} |||
|---|---|---|
| Number of Men | Equipment | Ammunition |
| 7 | Rifles and individual equipment | 136 rounds per rifleman 320 rounds per automatic rifle |
| 7 | 1 light machine gun | 10 boxes of ammunition |
| 7 | 1 heavy machine gun .30 caliber | 13 boxes of ammunition |
| 7 | 1 heavy machine gun .50 caliber | 13 boxes of ammunition |
| 7 | 1 81mm mortar | 24 rounds of ammunition |
| 7 | 1 60mm mortar | 36 rounds of ammunition |
| 0 | 1860 pounds of cargo. | |

Above: A June 1943 ad for Evinrude Outboard Motors showing Storm Boats in action.
(Author's collection)

the bow of the boat while the other engineer shoved the boat off before he took his position as operator. Then the motor operator knelt in the stern to operate the motor.

Some of the manufacturers of the boats were the Minnitonka Boat Works in Wayzola, Minnesota, the Pine Castle Boat and Construction Co. in Pine Castle, Florida and in Michigan were the Mainistee's Century Boat Co. and Charlevoix's Foster Boat Co.[15]

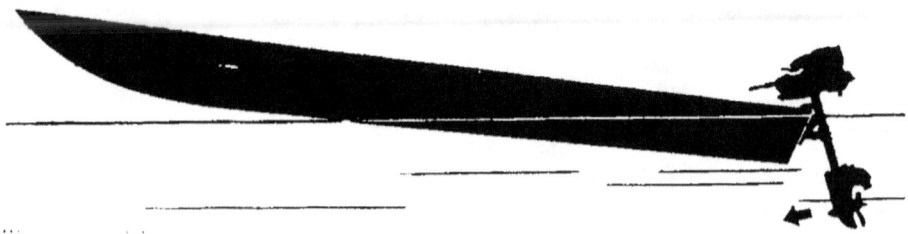

Above: the original caption says: where the propeller is tilted too far away from stern, bow is high in the water. (from
Below: a drawing of the U.S. Storm boat. Unfortunately, unlike the other boats in the book, I couldn't obtain even a photocopy of the original drawings. This is my best guess.

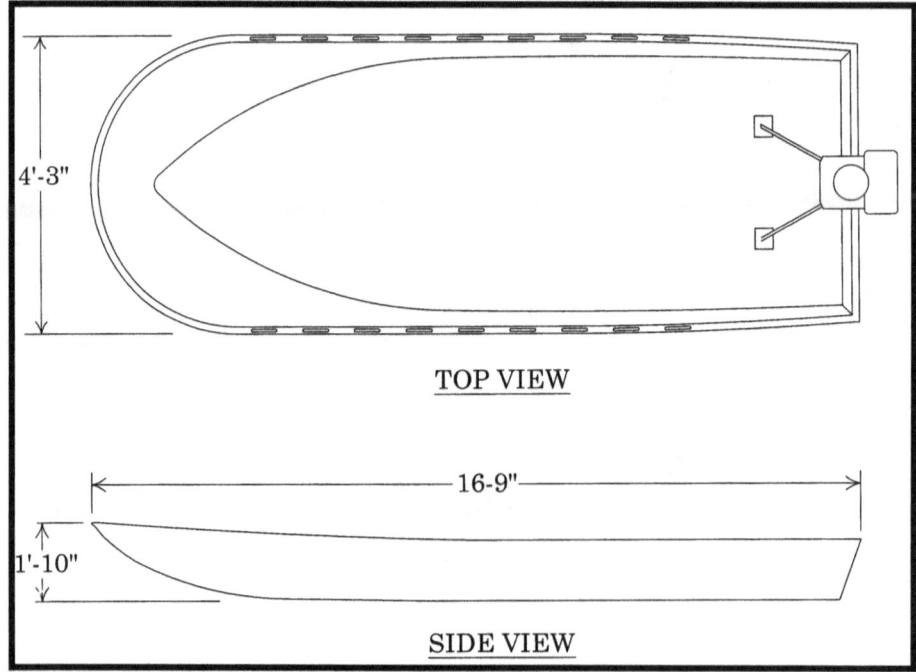

Above: German troops are being transported across a river on their version of the pneumatic floats. (author's collection)

## Pneumatic Floats

Inspired by the German use of rubber boats and rafting, the U.S. designed three sizes of pneumatic floats. They were the 6-ton, 10-ton (later 12) and the 25-ton. The largest sizes were used strictly for rafting and bridging.

The 6-ton pneumatic float was 20 feet long, 6 feet wide, and 2 feet deep. It was made of rubberized fabric and consisted of an outer tube, a floor, and a removable central tube. Each tube was 24 inches in diameter. The outer tube was divided by bulkheads into eight compartments, each with a separate inflation valve. Straps on the outer tube were used to secure a superstructure to the float when constructing expedient rafts or bridging.

The removable central tube was divided into two compartments. Tie-down straps held it in place. This central tube increased the rigidity of the float and maintained buoyancy when the float was submerged. It was normally removed when the float was used as a personnel carrier.

The float weighed approximately 375 pounds and had a maximum displacement of 12,000 pounds. It was carried folded in a canvas case 3 feet square by 18 inches deep. Included in each case was an emergency repair kit. Seven paddles in a canvas case were issued with each float.[17]

When not used for bridging, the 6-ton pneumatic float was employed either as a reconnaissance boat or as an assault boat in a river crossing. As an assault boat, it wasn't used in the first wave as it was too vulnerable to small arms fire. Instead it was used as a ferry to transport the follow-up waves. When used as a transport, the central tube was removed. It was advisable to lay planks on the flooring to prevent puncturing the fabric. The float could accommodate 15 men comfortably and 30 was the maximum number that could be crowded onboard.

It could also be used as a raft and as part of the 6-ton Pneumatic Pontoon bridge.

A lift line extended around the outside of the float; it was not used for carrying. D-rings were attached to the float for carrying and lashing purposes.

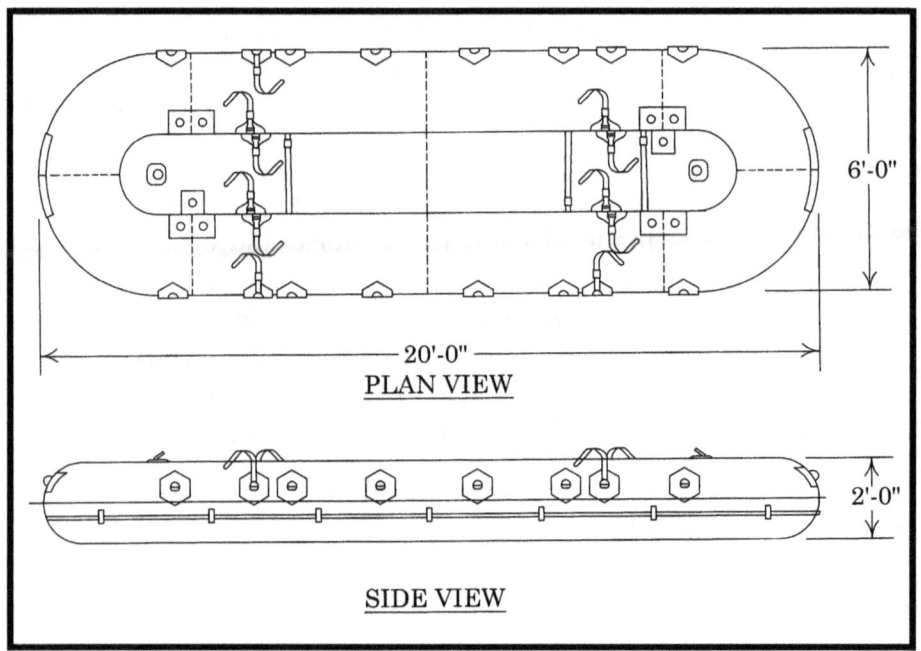

U.S. Pneumatic Float

# British And Commonwealth Boats

During the last stages of the First World War, the need for rapid bridging of tank obstacles in the British Army became a factor. It was at this time that a permanent home for the innovation and development of bridging equipment for the British Army was set up in the old cavalry and artillery barracks at Christchurch. It was the perfect spot for their task with the River Stour running through the camp and the tank proving grounds not too far away. At first the Experimental Bridging Company, Royal Engineers was made up of all Royal Engineers (R.E.) personnel, but would reform as the Experimental Bridging Establishment (E.B.E.) in 1925, consisting predominantly of civilians - one of them the famed Sir Donald Bailey, the inventor of the Bailey Bridging. Even with a large percentage of civilians it would retain a Royal Engineering Officer as its director until 1957 when it became known as the Military Engineering Experimental Establishment (M.E.X.E.). Its peak strength of workers during the war was around 500.[18]

Significant developments pertaining to infantry assault crossing equipment happened during a regatta at the E.B.E. in the late 1930s as Britain geared up for another world war. Seventeen boats of various designs were put through their paces and, in the end, only two designs were selected for production. One of these was the collapsible canvas Assault Boat. Thus the British Army entered the war with the Assault Boat as their main boat and, like the Americans, they weren't inspired to develop a Storm Boat until the Germans first used them in 1940.

At the beginning of the war, 48 Assault boats were part of an Infantry Division's Field Park Company and twenty-four were part of the Armoured Division's Field Park and in the Bridge Company RASC. This changed and by 1942 all Assault boats were carried by the Bridge Company for the rest of the war. The Bridge Company, R.A.S.C., was a Corps level unit that was responsible for the delivery and maintenance of the majority of the bridging equipment. A small amount of bridging equipment was held at divisional level, but this didn't include Assault or Storm

Boats. Eighty boats were carried in ten of the Bridge Company's trucks.

Storm Boats were carried in General Transport companies and weren't part of normal bridging operations. They nested three boats to a lorry. The engines and the accessories were also carried in the same truck.

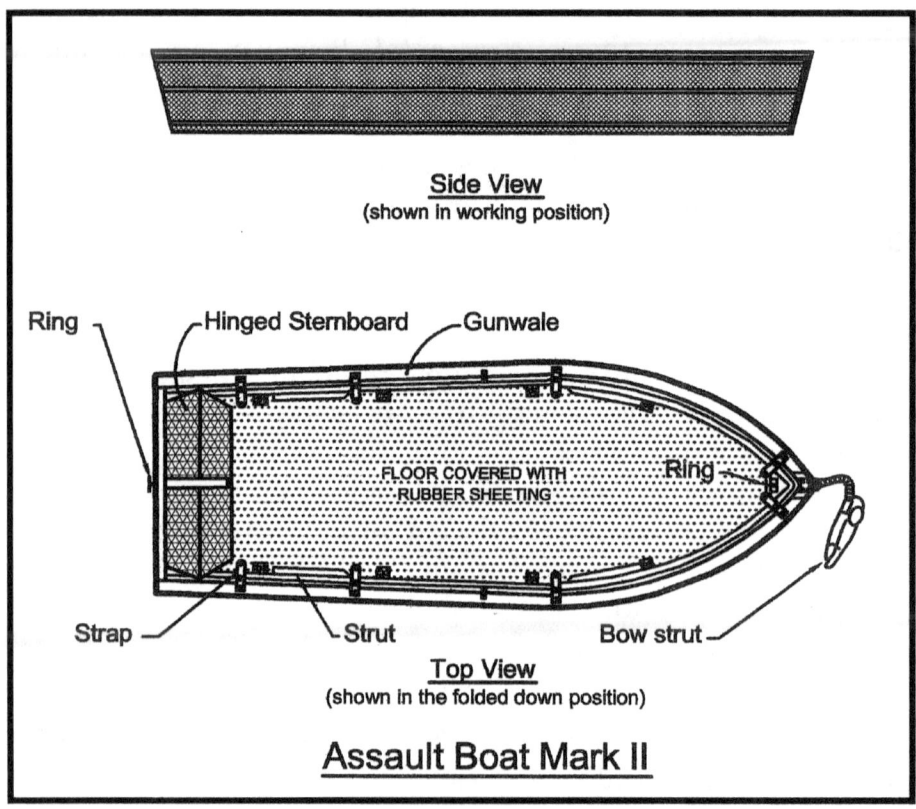

# British Assault Boat

The assault boat was a collapsible canvas boat that had a variety of uses. One use was to carry infantry silently across a waterway during an assault crossing where noise was a factor. Also, with special attachments, it could ferry an anti-tank gun across a river, act as floatation for carriers and as supports for a light floating bridge. The Mark I was 12'-1 ½" long, 4'-8" wide at its widest point and 1'-11" high at the bow when in the working position. It was made of a plywood floor, canvas sides and a stiff timber gunwale. The floor was lined with cedar grating that the men knelt on with one knee while in the boat. The sides were kept extended by means of four struts that locked into place. In this position, a crew of two - though it was strongly suggested that two additional rowers were selected from the passengers - could transport seven passengers across a river. To encourage this further, four paddles were provided for paddling or rowing and one was kept as a spare. A mooring pin and line were attached to the bow.[19]

For transportation the struts were unlocked and folded, allowing the sides to collapse down to four inches. The gunwale was held to the floor by means of four webbing straps and buckles. In either the open or closed position six men, spread out evenly along the sides to distribute the weight, could carry the boat.

A variation was made using a non-skid rubber floor for noise reduction while embarking. This was known as the Mark 1A. It soon gave way to the Mark II. The Mark II was basically the same as the Mark I, but with the same non-skid rubber floor as the Mark 1A. The boat was slightly different in size – at 12'-1 ½" long, 4'7" wide and was 1'-6" high throughout - and shape, but like the first, it also weighed 162 pounds.

The Royal Engineers entered the war with the Assault Boat Mark II as its assault crossing equipment, with the Folding Boat Equipment Mark II as a back-up. Even though the F.B.E. was really designed for bridging, it could be used to ferry men if needed. However, this role was highly discouraged as it took valuable resources from the rafting and bridging effort.

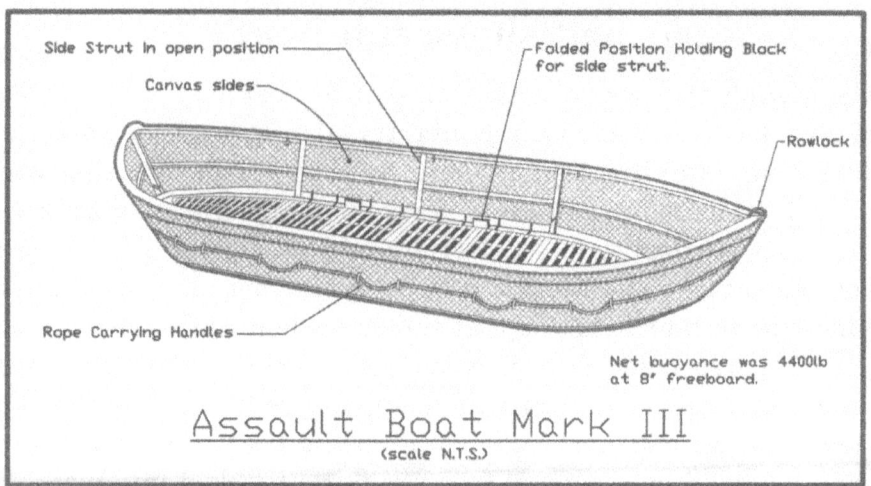

Assault Boat Mark III
(scale N.T.S.)

By 1944 production had caught up with demand and new types of equipment had been developed and implemented. The E.B.E. at Christchurch had been busy. The Assault Boat Mark II version was obsolete and was no longer being produced, though some were still being used. A naval-type assault boat replaced it. The Assault Boat Mark III was larger and more buoyant than its predecessors and had the advantage of its bow and stern being interchangeable so it could easily be hauled back and forth across a river by ferrying cables. This saved the necessity of having to turn the boat around and was the most efficient method of ferrying men and equipment across a river and was used whenever possible.

The Mark III was larger than the earlier models. The 16'-8" long and 5'-5" boat was designed to take the newly enlarged infantry section and a few of its support troops in one trip. The maximum capacity was 16 men plus a two-man crew, but this was unsafe except in completely smooth water. The normal operating capacity was 11 men, plus a two-man crew. [20]

The bottom of the boat was made of plywood and had an additional layer made of either rubber or slatted wood. Like its predecessors, the sides were canvas and the gunwale was made of stiff timber. At each end there was a rowlock for steering and a 17' breast line with a mooring spike was attached.

The equipment provided with the boat were eight paddles, one steering oar and an emergency repair set. Also 40 fathoms of 1

Above: an Assault Boat in the folded position, for ease of carrying. (National Archives and Library of Canada)

Below: Canadian Scottish training in a Mark III Assault Boat during a training exercise in the U.K.. (National Archives and Library of Canada)

½" cordage, 2-5' pickets and one maul could also be provided, depending on the task at hand. The extra equipment was carried along with the boat and its usual stores in the Assault Platoon of a Bridging Company.

It was recommended that the boat be opened out of earshot and sight of the enemy and that six men were usually assigned to carry it. The 350-pound boat could either be carried on the shoulder or by the rope handles and, like the previous versions, the carrying party should have been equally spread out along the sides to distribute the weight evenly.

Fully loaded the boat drew about 1'-6" to 1'-9" of water and therefore had to have been at this depth before embarkation began or the boat would have been grounded. Each man was given an assigned place in the boat where he knelt on one knee. The men who were selected to paddle gave their rifles to the men in the middle to hang on to while the boat was in motion.

An emergency repair set was capable of making minor repairs to the boat, but for any major repairs, the boat had to be sent back to the R.E. platoon of the Bridging Company, who were capable of resurrecting an almost completely destroyed boat.

Above: a typical loading diagram of the Assault Boat Mark III, showing the positioning of the crew and passengers. (from: Field Engineering and Mine Warfare Pamphlet No. 8 Part I (All arms) Assault River Crossing)

One such opportunity was the crossing of the Lamone River on December 10th, 1944 by the 11th Canadian Infantry Brigade. Starting at 1930 hours troops from the brigade quietly paddled over in assault boats while their Division's field guns distracted the enemy by shelling the flanks. At 2130 hours the 3rd Infantry Brigade crossed the same river in similar fashion, proving that the strength of these boats were how quiet they were to operate.

The assault crossing of the Waal River by members of the American 82nd Airborne Division highlighted the boat's main disadvantage. The paddled boats were slow moving targets on a wide, fast river and many lives were lost in that daylight crossing.

# Storm Boat Mark I

Another product of the E.B.E. was the Storm Boat Mark I. It was a large plywood boat designed to be used during an opposed crossing over a wide fast river and was still considered to be experimental in 1944, so much so that many senior RE officers were skeptical of them. The British 43rd Wessex Division's bloody crossing of the Seine River in Storm Boats only reinforced their opinion. They did not take into count that the problem was not the boats themselves, and these boats quickly proved to be invaluable in the right hands.

The 20' long boat with a 6'-6" beam was powered by the Evinrude #8008 outboard engine and was able to carry heavier and bigger loads faster than the paddle powered assault boats. The main disadvantage was that because of the motor, it created a lot of noise and thus alerted the enemy of its presence.

The Stormboat had an oak frame and its sides and bottom were made of plywood. The seat tracks – or benches – were made of oak and were fitted along the sides of the boat from the stern. They served either as seats or as ramps for the wheels of either an anti-tank gun or a jeep. Between the benches the flooring was hinged to facilitate bailing.

The boat, together with the motor and all of the onboard equipment, weighed roughly 1500 pounds and could reach speeds of 20 knots while empty and 6 knots when fully loaded. The maximum load was 35 cwt. That translated to 18 fully armed men, a jeep or a six-pounder anti-tank gun, plus crew. This included the boat's crew of two, consisting of a steersman and a bowman. According to an early war training manual the steersman was in command of the boat and operated the motor while the bowman was responsible for pushing off on departure and fending off on arrival. However, some units, like the 23rd Field Company, R.C.E. used a three-man crew consisting of a coxswain, boatman and a shoreman. Like the steersman, the coxswain was in command of the boat, including all passengers while they were on board, and operated the outboard motor. The boatman supervised the loading and trim of the boat, guided the boat while under way and assisted the shoreman during shoving off and fending off. He was

Allied Attack Boats

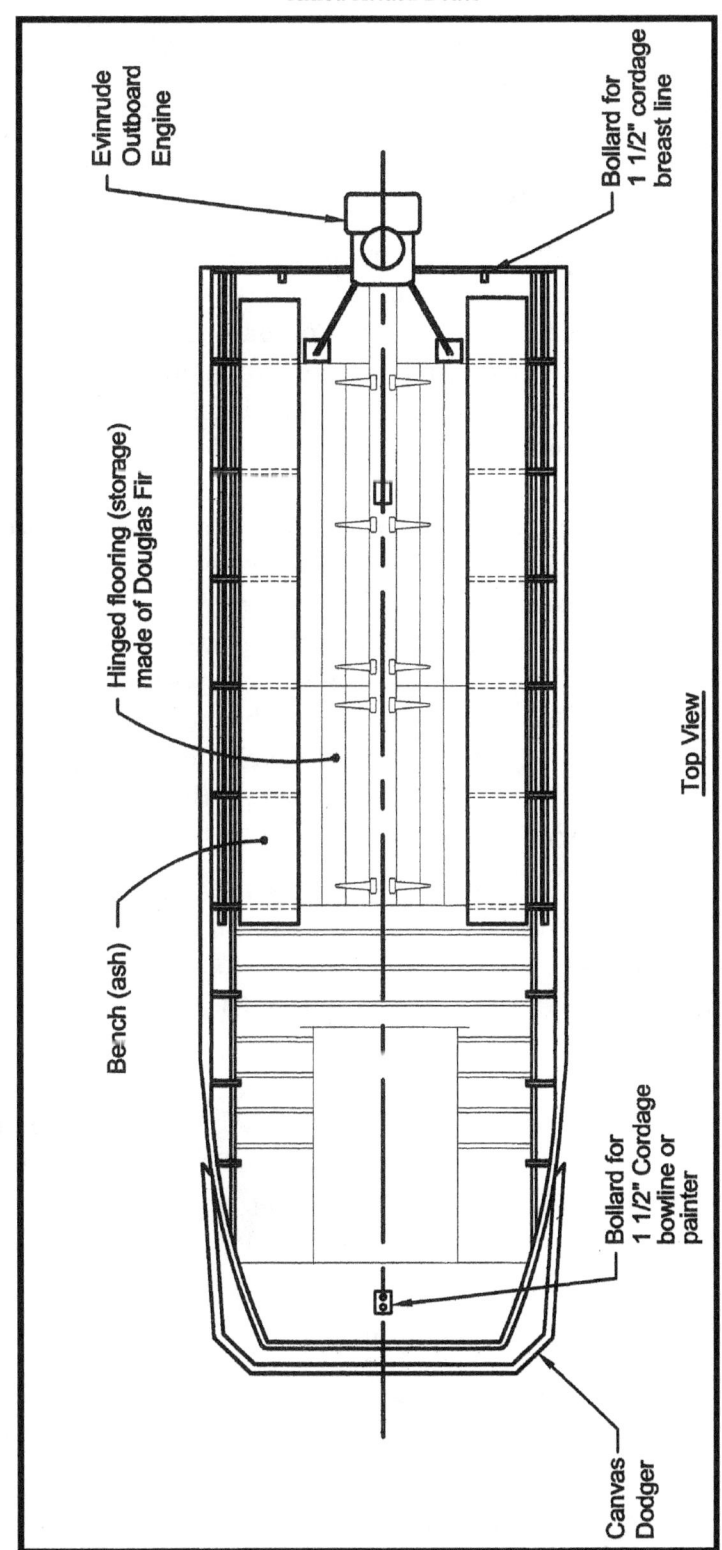

also responsible for spelling off the coxswain if needed. The shoreman was responsible for reporting to the section commander when each trip was completed, when fuel was low or if casualties occurred, for guiding passengers, for pushing off during departure and for fending off upon arrival.

Since a counterattack by the enemy usually included tanks it was essential that anti-tank guns get across soon after the initial assault. Tests by the 1st Field Park Company, R.C.E. proved that Storm Boats could be used to transport six-pounder guns. To facilitate this, steel ramps were provided for loading and off-loading of equipment on banks up to three feet in height. When loading and unloading the boat needed to be made secure by ropes fastened to pickets or trees on shore, especially when driving a jeep off the boat. To load a piece of equipment two steel tracks were fitted over the bow that rested with one end on the bench and the other end on the bank. The six-pounder anti-tank gun was loaded muzzle first and the correct position was for the axle of the gun to sit 6'-1" forward of the outside of the stern transom. The crew would sit on the bench, forward of the gun. The position of the jeep was determined so that its rear wheels were just on the bench.

Wheel chocks were provided to ensure that the gun or jeep did not move during the crossing. The maximum load when carrying infantry in calm water was approximately 35 cwts and when carrying guns or jeeps it was approximately 31 cwts. The top speed when loaded with 18 infantrymen or a six-pounder anti-tank gun with crew was 7-½ m.p.h. This got slightly better with the two-pounder anti-tank gun (9 m.p.h.) and with a jeep (10 m.p.h.). Less men to carry meant higher speeds and the boat could reach 11 m.p.h. with only 12 men and 15½ m.p.h. when that number was cut down to 8. Empty, except for the two-crew members, the boat topped out at 25-½ m.p.h.

One Storm Boat Mark I Set comprised of:

| # - Piece Of Equipment | Weight |
|---|---|
| 1 x storm boat complete canvas dodger and fittings for attaching an outboard engine and ramps | 900 lb. |
| 2 x steel trough ramps (165 lbs. each) | 330 lb. |

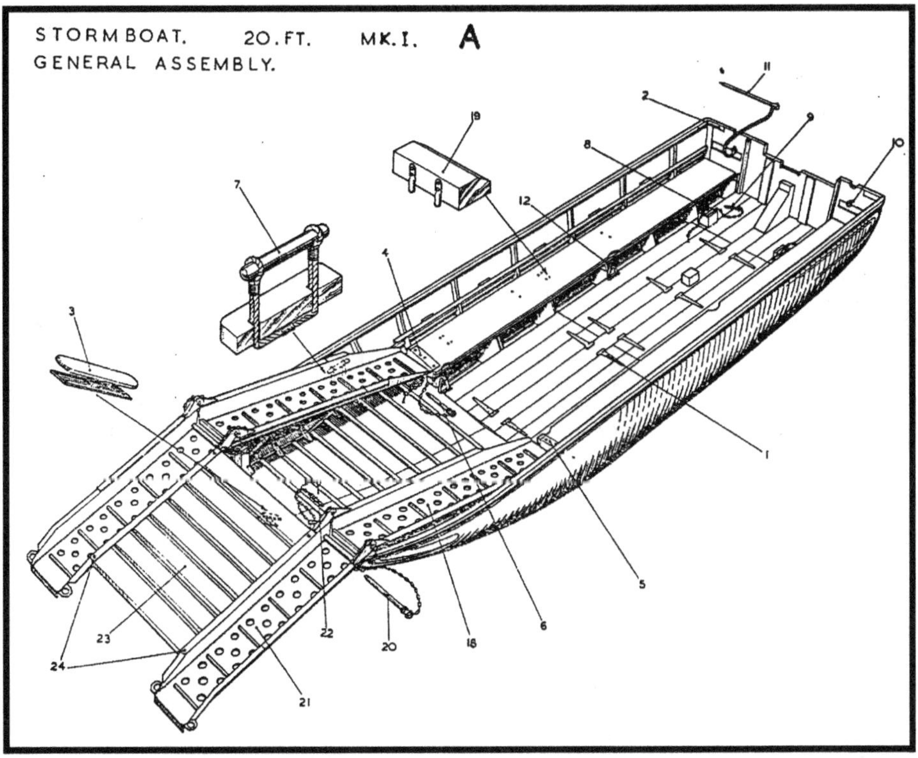

## Allied Attack Boats

STORMBOAT. 20. FT. MK. I. A
GENERAL ASSEMBLY.

Above: an isometric drawing of a Storm boat with all of its accessories, but without the motor. The ramp allowed the loading and unloading of jeeps and anti-tank guns. (NAL) Below: members of the Royal Canadian Engineers maneuver a Storm Boat towards a river. (PA138285)

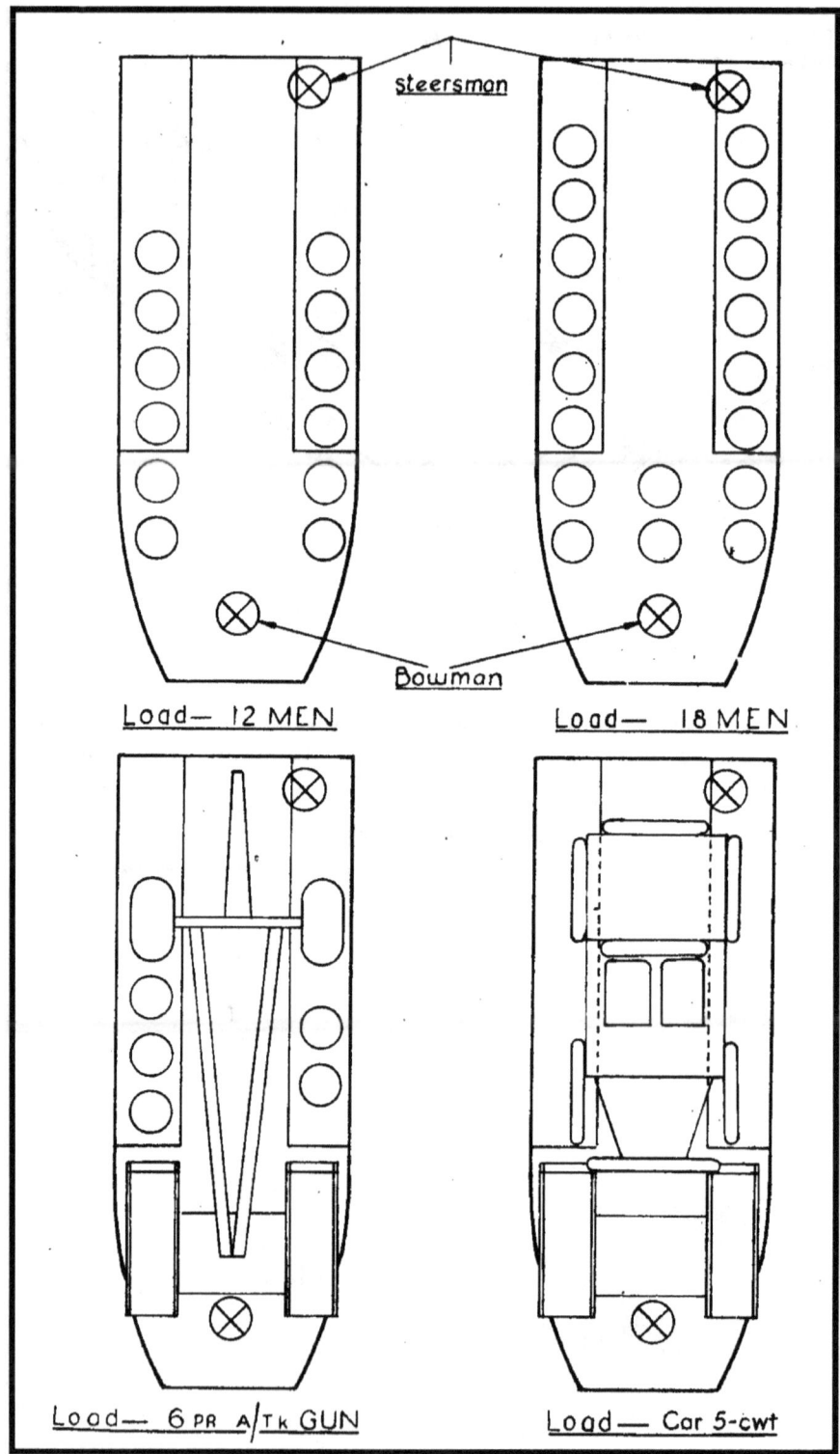

Above: a sketch from Rafting and Bridging showing the loads of a Storm Boat. (NAL)

| | |
|---|---|
| 1 x timber foot walk | 50 lb. |
| 4 x wheel chocks (6 lbs each) | 24 lb. |
| 1 x 50 H.P. Evinrude outboard engine model 8008 complete with tools and accessories | 198 lb. |
| 4 x 2 gallon petrol cans filled with petrol/oil mixture | 80 lb. |
| 1 x 7 lb. sledge | 9 lb. |

The canvas dodgers folded under the gunwale when the ramps were in use to prevent the intake of water in the bow. The wheel chocks sat on the benches to prevent the wheels of the guns and jeeps from moving while the boat was in motion. Other attachments to the boat included a 10' boat hook, two breast lines with spikes attached (that were secured to the ring bolts in the stern transom), and a mop.[21]

## The Storm boat in Review

In early May 1945 Lt-Col W.W. K. McConnell, the SORE 1 Ops Officer at the HQ of First Canadian Army sent out a survey entitled 'Lessons Of The Campaign In NW Europe 1944-45' to its senior engineers. The reason for this is stressed in his first point: *'It is of the greatest importance that the lessons of the campaign as far as they concern org, eqpt and technique of the Royal Canadian Engrs are now considered and recorded before the offrs, who have had the practical experience are scattered'.* One of the question concerned river crossings and the equipment used for it. It asked, *'Is the Stormboat and 50 HP motor still required in its present form, or in any other form?'*

The following are their responses:

Brigadier D.K. Black, CE of 2 Cdn Corps: *'A very valuable piece of eqpt if the engine were more reliable'.*

Lt-Col V.C. Hamilton, CRE 2 Cdn C Tps: *'The stormboat in its present form and the 50 HP motor with a clutch are required, the reason for the latter being that the stormboat is an excellent load carrier but it is necessary to shut off the motor to disembark troops because the prop picks up weeds close to shore and the shore crew have difficulty shoving the boat off for the return trip. It usually takes a considerable time to start the motor again, hence the need for a clutch.'*

Lt-Col E.W. Henselwood, CRE 2 Cdn Inf Div: *'The present 50HP motor is too temperamental. A more rugged and reliable motor is required. The Storm boat is satisfactory.'*

Lt-Col J.R.B. Jones, CRE 4 Cdn Armd Div: *'It is still required for wide or fast rivers. It is very awkward to handle in carrying or transporting by truck'.*

Major T.M. Kingsbury, OC 18 Cdn Fd Coy: *'The stormboat is a necessary part of assault eqpt. It should be provided with carrying handles. The 50 HP Evinrude is too tempermental and a sturdier motor is required.*[22]

Allied Attack Boats

# Motors

An outboard motor is a power plant complete with engine, gasoline supply and starting apparition and was easily installed and detached from the boat. All outboard motors have a powerhead, an engine, a drive shaft extending downward into the water to drive the propeller, and a propeller.

The powerhead consists of the cylinders, crankscase, crankshaft, pistons and connecting-rod assemblies, muffler, magneto system, carburetor and fuel tank. Its engine supplied power to drive the propeller in the other main part. The lower unit transmitted engine power to the propeller and included the transmission gears, drive and propeller shafts, bearings, water pump, exhaust outlet and mounting bracket.

The outboard motors used by the U.S. Army operated on the two-stroke cycle principle, each cylinder having one port for intake and one for exhaust. Two-cycle engines were considerably lighter per unit of power output than the four-cycle, since they have fewer parts and every piston has a power stroke at each revolution instead of every other revolution. Light weight and compact size in an outboard motor are of prime importance for ease in carrying, attaching and operating.

Elementary Outboard Motor Operation (from "Outboard Motors"

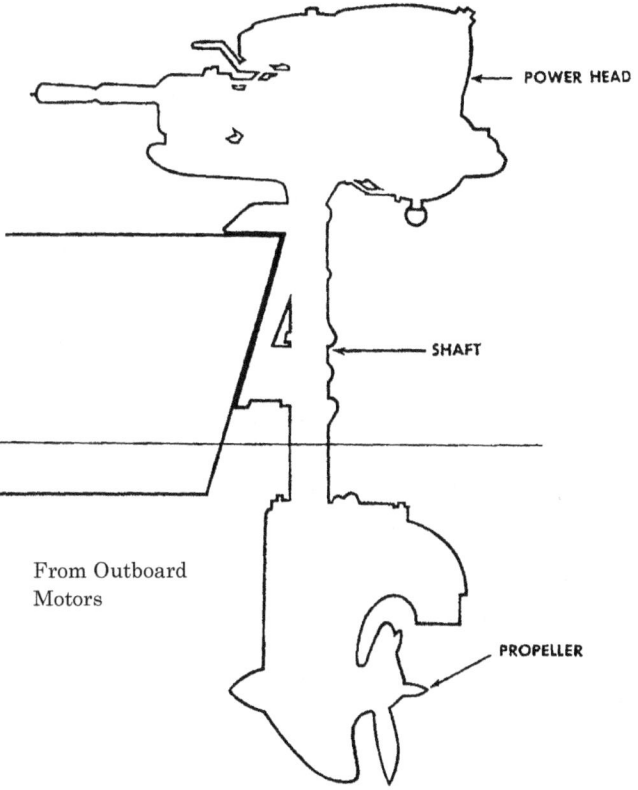

From Outboard Motors

A) STEERING. Steering is done with the left hand. The operator faces the bow of the boat with the motor to his left as shown in figure 31. The craft is steered by moving the steering handle to the right or left. If the operator wishes to make the boat turn to the left, he moves the handle toward him, or to the right. To make a right turn he moves the handle away from him, or to the left. The motor pivots so the diection of boat travel is governed by the propeller thrust. This gives the operator full control of the boat from the time the motor is started.

B) DOCKING. In docking, the boat is brought in parallel to the dock, if possible, heading into the wind or current, whichever has the greater effect on the boat's course. In docking where the landing room is limited, the boat is brought toward the dock at a right angle to it. A short distance form the dock a 90 degree turn into the wind or current is made and the motor shut off. The boat will drift broadside into the dock. The distance from the dock at which the turn is made depends on the type of boat and the speed it is making.

C) REVERSE. The POLR-15 can be pivoted 360 degrees. It is reversed by raising the steering handle and turning the motor 180 degrees to reverse position. The speed of the motor should be reduced before pivoting the motor to the reverse position. The motor does not tilt when in reverse, so particular care must be taken to avoid striking submerged obstructions.

D) BEACHING STORM BOAT. The boat may be beached at full throttle on banks having gentle slopes. The motor is stopped by the operator immediately before the skeg or the bow of the boat grounds. This depends on the depth of water near the bank. The boat must be headed directly into the beach so the bow will ground squarely. If the boat slants as it grounds, it will swerve and possibly tilt over.[23]

The Royal Engineers did not beach their version of the Storm boat in the same manner. Their beaching method was more gentle.

## Johnson Sea-Horse POLR-15

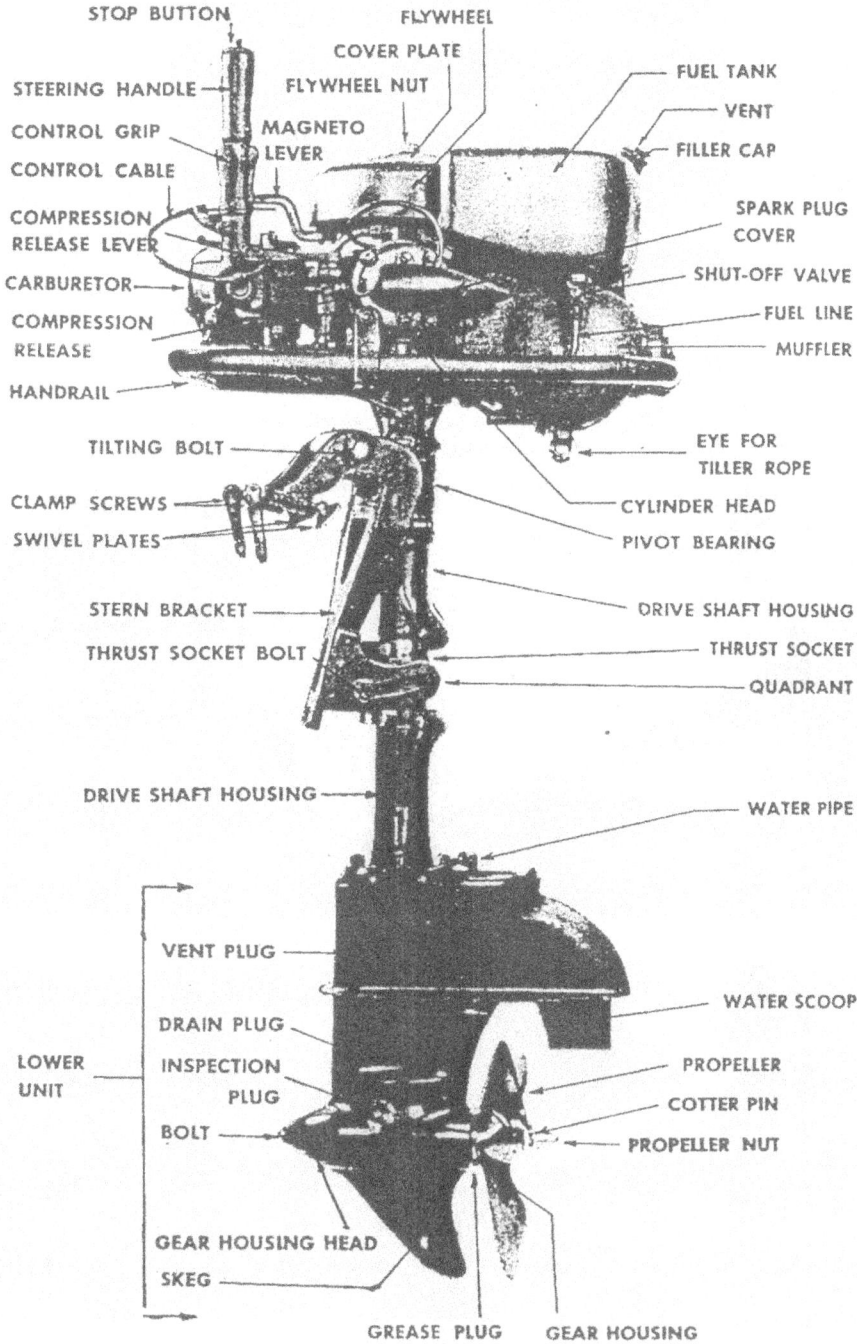

Above: From the manual on the Johnson 22hp or POLR-15 outboard motor.

The 22 hp motor weighed 126 pounds and was made for fresh water applications. It was started by a rope starter and a magneto ignition. It was open exhaust and cooled by a pressure vacuum cooling system. It had a 10 inch three blade propeller, full pivot steering and a reverse gear.

To start, one pint of SAE No. 40 lubricating oil was mixed with each gallon of gasoline before the tank was filled.

It was used primarily by the U.S. Army and normally attached to the M2 Assault boat with a '*M2 Assault Boat, 22-hp outboard motor stern attachment bracket*'. The bracket could also be used on the 10-ton and 25-ton pontoons. The motor worked better when it was used with the double assault boat configuration instead of the single configuration.[24]

Above: A Johnson motor on a Assault Boat M2. (Philip Reinders)

# Motor, Outboard, 50 H.P., Model 8008,

The motor that propelled both the British and the U.S. versions of the storm boat was an American made Evinrude Model #8008 Outboard Engine. It was a 50 H.P. 2 stroke engine that weighed 198 pounds. The motor sat on the stern transom and was supported on the apex of an A-frame, to which the legs were attached inside. This arrangement allowed for the motor to be quickly brought onboard if necessary. The vertical shaft was hinged on the transom bracket so that the motor tilted on striking the riverbed in shallow water. It was cooled by a centrifugal pump and had an underwater exhaust. The fuel for this engine was 1 gallon of petrol thoroughly mixed with one pint of SAE 50

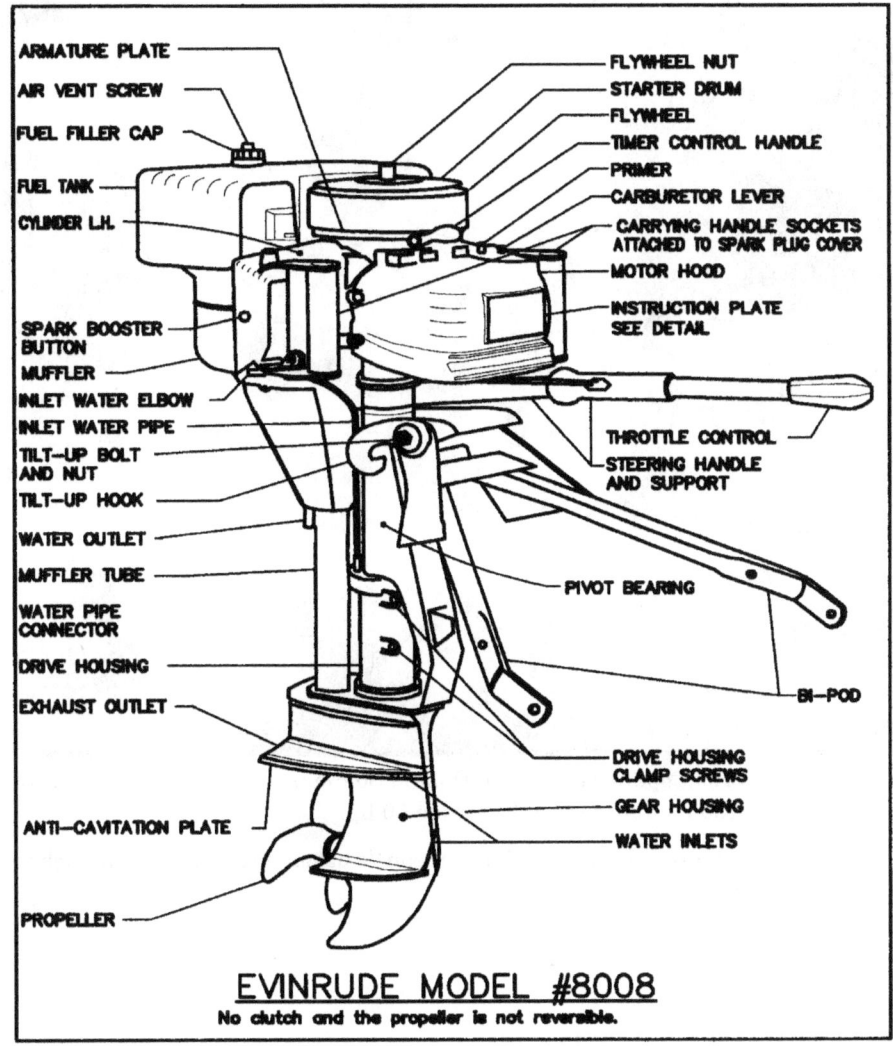

Above: Storm Boat operator veteran, Donald Sommerville and an outboard collector look at the manual for the Evinrude 50 hp.

The motor on the stand was found in someone's basement and brought back to working condition.

(photo taken by author)

or M400 oil and it was consumed at four to five gallons per hour at full speed. It had a 3-½ gallon fuel tank and the four extra fuel cans were stored under the benches. It had no clutch, a 90 degree steering angle and the 10 ¾" propeller was not reversible. [25]

Pulling a rope started the engine, but this was not always successful, especially if the spark plugs got wet. A good example of this happening (or more accurately the motors not happening) was during the evacuation of the British 1st Airborne Division by the 20th and 23rd Field Companies, R.C.E. on September 25th/26th 1944. The heavy rain soaked the engines and many of them had to be abandoned. One time in particular almost had disastrous consequences for Lieutenant Russ Kennedy of the 23rd Field Company, R.C.E. It was almost daylight when he found himself in an overloaded boat with an engine that would not start. He kept pulling, but the engine would not start. They were on the north side of the river and if he could not get the motor going then all of them would be prisoners and/or killed by the approaching Germans. Fortunately, after dozens of tries, the motor started and he was able to cross back to his unit. It was reported that 36 men had been crammed into the boat. Lieutenant Kennedy comments on how packed the boat was: *"I barely had room to pull the chord to start the engine. Everytime I did a wave of men would fall back to stay clear of my arm."* [26]

The general consensus of the motor can be summed up in the Twenty-Third Story: *"The motors are very powerful, but we find them most unreliable except under very favourable conditions"* [27]

After their experience at Arnhem, the 23rd submitted a report on how to waterproof the Evinrude engines and after testing, Colonel C.J. Bermingham, the CO of 1 Canadian Army Group Royal Engineers, submitted a report entitled, `Waterproofing and Modification Of Evinrude Outboard Motor'. The 26 October 1944 report states that the engines that were not waterproofed had only a 50% chance of starting during wet conditions and that the engines with the recommended waterproofing had a 90% chance of starting. Also, the effects of a wave over the stern had no effect on the treated engines. The untreated engines stalled and would not start again until they were dried out.[28]

Above: The Evinrude motor. (taken by Author)

**INSTRUCTIONS**

1. MIX ONE PINT #50 OIL WITH EACH GALLON OF GASOLINE, BEFORE FILLING TANK.
2. OPEN VENT SCREW (ON TANK CAP).
3. OPEN GAS COCK UNDER TANK (TOWARD YOU).
4. SET CARBURETOR LEVER TO COLD.
5. SET TIMER TO START.
6. SET STEERING GRIP TO START.
7. WRAP ROPE ON FLYWHEEL.
8. PUSH PRIMER FIVE TIMES.
9. SPIN FLYWHEEL WITH STRONG PULLS
10. WHEN STARTED MOVE TIMER AT ONCE TO RUN, ALSO TURN STEERING GRIP TOWARD FAST.
11. WITH THROTTLE WIDE OPEN ADJUST CARB. LEVER TOWARD WARM UNTIL MOTOR RUNS SMOOTHLY.
12. IF MOTOR IS HOT PRIME SPARINGLY.
13. STOP MOTOR BY MOVING TIMER HANDLE ALL THE WAY TO LEFT.
14. USE CHAMPION R-7 SPARK PLUGS.

EVINRUDE MOTOR, MILWAUKEE, WIS., U.S.A.

**INSTRUCTION PLATE DETAIL**

Above: the instructions on the front of the Evinrude motor.

## Seagull Engine

The type of engine that was most often used with F.B.E. and could also be used with the Assault Boat Mk. III was the 'Seagull Engine'. It was rated at 3 ½ to 4 hp. Made in England by British Seagull Inc., a company born out of Marston Seagull in 1938 in

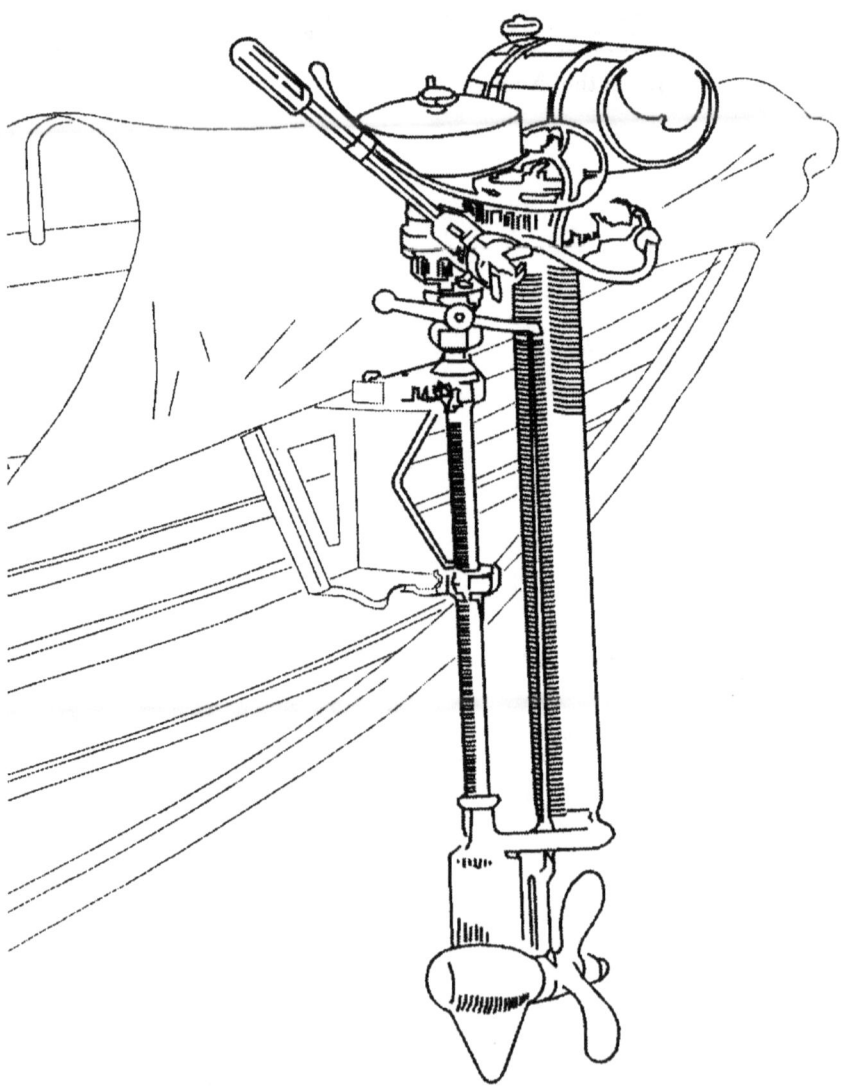

Above: Seagull Mark III attached to F.B.E. Drawn by author from a PAM.

Quay at Poole, Dorset. At the time they claimed that it was the best outboard motor in the world.

The owners of the company thought that reverse gears were a `a rather sissy refinement, rendered superfluous by efficient boat handling' to quote John Way-Hope off their website. Instead, they patented a `Positive and Self-Adjusting Free-Engine Clutch' that remained basically unchanged for the next twenty years. The company believes that the Admiralty's request for a `rough and ready' version of the `102' for use on light assault craft, that could run non-stop for 24 hours, helped establish the company. Their existing engine needed few alterations to fulfill their needs. It was known as the 102 plus.[30]

The Ministry of Supply printed "Outboard Motor Set, Seagull Mark II: Provisional Working Instructions' and it described the composition of a set comprising of:

a) *trade pattern "Seagull" outboard motor, fully silenced with 10" diameter propeller complete with starting cord and handle, developing 3 ½-4 B.H.P. at 4000 RPM;*

b) *gunmetal boat bracket for fixing (a) to either side of folding boat, Mark III.*

c) lists all of the accessories to be included such as tool pouch, grease gun, combined magneto spanner and feeler, jet key and timing spanner, canvas cover for engine and P.W.T.

d) lists the spare parts to be carried and

e) lists all of the transport cases to carry all of the above. The single cylinder, two stroke engine weighed 47 pounds was 4'-2" in depth and tests proved that one Seagull engine could power a F.B.E. with a 2750 pound payload up to 4. 5 knots.[29]

Three views of the Seagull. (all three photos taken by author)

Above left: a side view of the Seagull. The stern of the boat would be to the right of the motor.

Above right: an end view of the Seagull.

Right: the operator's view of the Seagull.

# Conclusion

During the war, the majority of engineering equipment was pooled to alleviate supply problems but throughout the war Britain and the United States each preferred to use their own versions of attack boats and rarely used the other country's equipment. The exception was the Storm Boat engine, which was used by both countries.

Towards the end of the war amphibious vehicles like the Buffalos were used more often in river assaults replacing the unprotected Assault and Storm Boats, thus reducing casualties. Unfortunately, they arrived in too few numbers to support every crossing. However, there were still operations where having a light Assault Boat was preferable to a large noisy Amphibious vehicle. One example happened at Leer, where the infantry of the North Nova Scotia Highlanders carried British Assault Boats Mark III to the river and slipped relatively silently across the Leda River, surprising the Germans.

Both country's paddled boats functioned well when used to "slip" silently across a narrow river or canal and they both were used as part of a ferry and in forming bridging, though the British preferred to used the F.B.E. and pontoons. Even though the U.S. Assault Boat M2 was more robust (and harder to carry to the water as a result) and the canvas on the British Assault Boat Mark III had the tendency to catch fire when hit, I slightly favour the latter because the British boat could be efficiently pulled back and forth across a waterway without having to turn the boat around. This would result in a much higher rate of delivery of men and/or supplies. While this was happening, the U.S. Assault Boat M2 could be paired up to form pontoons for their Treadway Bridge.

The U.S. Storm Boat carried less men, but got them across a river more quickly. The British were slower, but could carry

Note: the Pneumatic floats and the F.B.E. were both regarded as bridging material that could be used to transport troops so to rate them in the assault role would be unfair.

heavier loads like jeeps and anti-tank guns while the U.S. version could not. Maybe the best case scenario for a direct assault using boats over a wide river might have the first wave in U.S. Storm Boats and race them at top speed to beach onto the far bank. Behind them British Storm Boats would carry the follow up waves with the heavier equipment, such as anti-tank guns.

Whatever the pros and cons of each boat, both countries found a way to utilize the strengths of their boats which resulted in numerous successful assault crossings during the campaign in North-west Europe that won the war against Germany. These boats represented in this book are part of that history.

## End Notes

1. p57-58 Engineers in Battle
2. River Crossing Technique, First Research Course, Vol. I, p25
3. p48 (Tech)
4. The Rhine Crossing Twelfth Army, Group Engineer Operations by General P.H. Timothy.
5. p99 The Technical Services
6. Military River-Crossing Equipment
7. Infantry School Mailing List Vol. 24, July 1942, p177.
8. p115 Engineer Soldier's Handbook
9. p182-184 The Mailing List / p9 Light Stream Crossing Eq.
10. p178-181 'The Mailing List'
11. Light Stream-crossing Equipage
12. Light Stream-crossing Equipage
13. Military River-Crossing Equipment
14. Engineer Soldier's Handbook / Military River Crossing Equipment
15. Article 'Wood At War.'
16. Light Stream-Crossing Equipage
17. Light Stream-Crossing Equipage
18. Military Engineering At Christchurch Barracks
19. Rafting and Bridging MTP No. 74
20. Rafting and Bridging MTP No. 74
21. Provisional Working Instructions For Storm Boat 20ft MK.I.
22. Lessons of the Campaign in NW Europe 1944-45
23. Outboard Motors
24. Outboard Motors
25. TM5-8010 / Outboard Motors
26. Whispers and Shadows
27. The Twenty-Third Story
28. Waterproofing and Modification of Evinrude Outboard Motor
29. Outboard Motor Set, Seagull Mark II / Rafting and Bridging / The British Seagull Operating Instructions
30. The British Seagull Operating Instructions

## References:

'United States Army In World War II: The Technical Services: The Corps Of Engineers: Troops And Equipment' by Blanche D. Coll, Jean E. Keith and Herbert H. Rosenthal. Office Of The Chief Of Military History Department Of The Army, Washington, D.C. 1958.

'Engineers In Battle' by Paul W. Thompson. The Military Service Publishing Company. June 1942

'Military Engineering At Christchurch Barracks' by John Barker

'Engineers in a River Crossing' from Infantry School Mailing List Volume 24, July 1942 pp 177-196

TB ENG 31 War Department Technical Bulletin 'Stream Crossing In High velocity Currents' 30 June 1944

'Rafting And Bridging. MTP No. 74. Part II and III.' Ministry of Supply. 1944

'The Rhine Crossing Twelfth Army Group Engineer Operations' by General P.H. Timothy

'Outboard Motor Set "Seagull" Mark II'. Ministry of Supply. 1942

'The British Seagull Operating Instructions' 24th Edition. The British Seagull Co. Ltd.

'Provisional Working Instructions for Storm Boat 20ft. Mk I' Ministry of supply. August 1944

TM 5-271 'Light Stream-crossing Equipage' War Department. April 10, 1943

FM-21-105 'Engineer Soldier's Handbook'. War Department. 2 June 1943

TM 5-278 'Outboard Motors' War Department. 30 June 1944

TM 5-801- 'Motor, Outboard, 50 H.P. Model 8008, 5in Shaft Extension' War Department. Feb 4, 1943

'Whispers and Shadows: Arnhem 50 Years Later' by Russell Kennedy

Article: 'Wood At War'.

ST 5-260-1B 'Military River Crossing Equipment' U.S. Army Engineer School, Fort Belvoir, Virginia, March 1955

Report: 'Lessons Of The Campaign In NW Europe 1944-45' CE HQ First Canadian Army 12 May 45

'The Twenty-Third Story' by Mike Tucker and the 23rd Fd. Coy. RCE

Report: 'Waterproofing and Modification of Evinrude Outboard Motor' Colonel C.J. Bermingham

## About The Author

John Sliz became fascinated with Operation Market Garden after he read, `A Bridge Too Far' at the age of nine. Many years later, a visit to Arnhem in the summer of 2001 only added fuel to the fire, eventually resulting in the publication of his first book, `The Storm Boat Kings'. While researching this book and waiting for its publication, he wrote a small booklet on the engineer equipment that was used during the operation. `Engineer Assault Boats In Canadian Service' was published in December 2006.

Since then he has written the first seven books of the Market Garden Engineer Series. He currently lives in Toronto, Ontario and is busy researching engineers in World War II. For more information or to contact him please visit: www.stormboatkings.ca

### Other Military Books By The Same Author

By Vanwell Publishing: (www.vanwell.com)
*The Storm Boat Kings:* The 23rd Royal Canadian Engineers At Arnhem 1944

By Service Publications: (www.servicepub.com)
*Non-Bailey Bridging In Canadian Service*
*Engineer Assault Boats In Canadian Service*
*The Bailey Bridge In Canadian Service (coming soon)*

Market Garden Engineer Series: (www.stormboatkings.ca)
#1) *The Wrong Side Of The River:* The Polish Engineer Company At Arnhem
#2) *Basic Function:* The 4th Parachute Squadron, Royal Engineers At Arnhem
#3) *Engineers At The Bridge:* The 1st Parachute Squadron Royal Engineers At Arnhem
#4) *Assault Boats On The Waal:* The 307th Engineer Battalion During Operation Market Garden
#5) *Bridging Hell's Highway:* The 326th Engineer Battalion During Operation Market Garden
#6) *A Long Tradition:* The 9th (Airborne) Field Company Royal Engineers At Arnhem
#7) *A Token Force:* The 261st Field Park Company Royal Engineers (Airborne) At Arnhem

www.ingramcontent.com/pod-product-compliance
Lightning Source LLC
Chambersburg PA
CBHW071757040426
42446CB00012B/2597